THE GREAT BOOKS FOUNDATION
Discussion Guide *for* Teachers

WE THE PEOPLE

About Perfection Learning

Founded by two educators, Perfection Learning is a family-owned company that has provided innovative, effective reading, literature, and language arts materials to K–12 classroom teachers for more than eighty-five years. The company offers two flagship literature programs, *Literature & Thought* and *Many Voices,* through its partnership with the Great Books Foundation. Each program uses engaging, thought-provoking literature selections to teach middle and high school students to be critical readers and thinkers. Each anthology is structured to help students explore essential questions and develop the skills necessary to be successful in the twenty-first century.

About the Great Books Foundation

The Great Books Foundation is an independent, nonprofit educational organization whose mission is to empower readers of all ages to become more reflective and responsible thinkers. To accomplish this, the Foundation teaches the art of civil discourse through Shared Inquiry™ and publishes enduring works of literature across the disciplines.

The Great Books Foundation was established in 1947 to promote liberal education for the general public. In 1962, the Foundation extended its mission to children with the introduction of Junior Great Books®. Since its inception, the Foundation has helped thousands of people throughout the United States and in other countries begin their own discussion groups in schools, libraries, and community centers. Today, Foundation instructors conduct hundreds of professional learning courses for teachers and parents each year, and Great Books programs help more than one million students learn to read, discuss, and appreciate some of the world's most enduring literature. Great Books programs combine classroom materials and the Shared Inquiry method of learning to provide the essential elements that students need to meet and surpass the goals of the Common Core State Standards for English Language Arts.

THE GREAT BOOKS FOUNDATION
Discussion Guide *for* Teachers

WE THE PEOPLE
FOUNDATIONS OF
AMERICAN GOVERNMENT

Perfection Learning

The Great Books Foundation
A nonprofit educational organization

Shared Inquiry™ is a trademark of the Great Books Foundation. Junior Great Books® is a registered trademark of the Great Books Foundation. The contents of this publication include proprietary trademarks and copyrighted materials and may be used or quoted only with permission and appropriate credit to the Foundation.

Copyright © 2012 by The Great Books Foundation
Chicago, Illinois
All rights reserved.
ISBN 978-1-933147-91-8

First printing
1 2 3 4 5 6 PP 17 16 15 14 13 12
Printed in the United States of America

Published and distributed by

The Great Books Foundation
A nonprofit educational organization

35 East Wacker Drive, Suite 400
Chicago, IL 60601

www.greatbooks.org

Contents

ABOUT SHARED INQUIRY AND THIS GUIDE	7
SCHEDULING SHARED INQUIRY ACTIVITIES	8
CONDUCTING SHARED INQUIRY ACTIVITIES	10
Prereading	10
First Reading	10
Sharing Questions	11
Second Reading	12
Shared Inquiry Discussion	14
Writing After Discussion	17
ASSESSMENT AND REFLECTION	18
SELECTIONS	
REAGAN'S FAREWELL ADDRESS *speech* Ronald Reagan	20
RELIGIOUS TOLERANCE IN AMERICA *essay* Richard Rodriguez	22
GIVE ME LIBERTY OR GIVE ME DEATH! *speech* Patrick Henry	24
DECLARATION OF INDEPENDENCE *primary source* Thomas Jefferson	26
THE FEDERALIST PAPERS *essay* James Madison	28
WHAT WOULD THE FOUNDERS DO? *book* Richard Brookhiser	30
WHY I HATE POLITICS. THAT GOVERNMENT KIND. *humor* Marcy Massura	32
WHY I'M POLITICAL *essay* Margaret Cho	34

REPRODUCIBLE FORMS

Shared Inquiry Discussion Guidelines	36
Building Your Answer in Shared Inquiry Discussion	38
Great Books Critical Thinking Rubric	40

About Shared Inquiry and This Guide

Welcome! This discussion guide for *We the People: Foundations of American Government* features a selection of texts that the Great Books Foundation recommends for close reading, text-based discussion, and evidence-based writing. Great Books programs use a method of interpretive reading and discussion known as Shared Inquiry,™ which complements the critical thinking encouraged in *We the People*.

Shared Inquiry is fully supportive of Common Core State Standards in both pedagogy and content. In Shared Inquiry, the leader uses open-ended questioning to help participants reach their own conclusions about challenging literature. The suggested sequence of activities—reading and asking questions, rereading and making notes, and exploring possible interpretations in discussion—mirrors the process that effective readers use with any complex text. Using Shared Inquiry, students develop the intellectual flexibility to analyze ideas and see a question from many angles. The focus on interpretation and discussion allows students at different reading levels to participate confidently and improve their critical thinking abilities.

This discussion guide includes general information about leading Shared Inquiry discussion and activities for eight selections from *We the People*. For each selection, you will find a prereading question, a note prompt for the second reading, suggested discussion questions, and prompts for writing after discussion. Also included are reproducible student handout pages for use in discussion and a rubric to assess critical thinking.

> **Professional Learning and Online Resources**
>
> The Great Books Foundation offers a range of professional learning opportunities, including online course options and on-site consultation days tailored to individual teachers' and schools' needs. To learn more, visit < www.greatbooks.org > or call 800-222-5870.
>
> Free resources, including downloadable materials and videos of classroom discussions are available at < www.greatbooks.org/resources >. Anyone who has taken the core Great Books professional learning courses can visit the Teacher Leaders Club at < www.greatbooks.org/tlc > for assessment tools, podcasts, videos, and special offers on classroom materials.

SCHEDULING SHARED INQUIRY ACTIVITIES

In-class work on a Great Books discussion unit consists of:

- **Prereading, first reading, and sharing questions:** setting a context for reading, reading the selection aloud if possible, and identifying questions worth exploring
- **Second reading:** rereading the selection, making notes using a specific prompt, and comparing those notes with other students
- **Shared Inquiry discussion:** the central Great Books activity, in which questions about the meaning of the text are explored in depth
- **Writing after discussion:** helping students consolidate or extend their ideas about a text

The activities that lead up to Shared Inquiry discussion prepare students for the discussion by helping them develop ideas about the story and find evidence in the text to support those ideas. After the discussion, the writing activities help extend students' engagement with the text, giving them opportunities to synthesize and elaborate on their ideas.

Following are two sample weekly schedules. Longer selections may require more in-class sessions, and some activities can be assigned as homework, depending on your students' needs and the time available.

Great Books and Common Core

Shared Inquiry provides the essential elements that students need to meet and surpass the goals of the Common Core State Standards. Great Books activities for *We the People*:

- Explore complex informational texts
- Require text-based answers
- Focus on evidence in writing
- Expand vocabulary
- Build knowledge across the curriculum

Option A: Three In-Class Sessions

Session 1

- Prereading activity (optional)
- First reading
- Sharing questions

Session 2

- Second reading
- Comparing and discussing notes

Session 3

- Shared Inquiry discussion

Homework: Writing after discussion

Option B: Two In-Class Sessions

Session 1

- First reading
- Sharing questions

Homework: Second reading

Session 2

- Comparing and discussing notes
- Shared Inquiry discussion

Homework: Writing after discussion

Conducting Shared Inquiry Activities

Preparing to Conduct Shared Inquiry Activities

As a Shared Inquiry leader, you serve as the model of an involved, curious thinker. We recommend that you prepare for Shared Inquiry by doing what your students will be doing: noting your own reactions and questions on a first reading, and marking the text using a specific note prompt on a second reading. Familiarizing yourself with the interpretive issues raised by the selection in this way will enable you to help your students develop their own ideas about the text as they participate in the sequence of Great Books activities.

Prereading 10–15 minutes *(optional)*

Activity Summary: Students briefly discuss a concept relevant to the text they will be reading.

Student Learning Objective: To activate prior knowledge and provide a context for understanding a text

The activities in this guide include a topic for a brief discussion before students read the text for the first time. A prereading discussion is especially helpful if the selection is challenging or the subject matter is unfamiliar to students. Keep prereading discussions short, since the goal is to spur students' interest in the text.

First Reading *(time depends on selection length)*

Activity Summary: Students read the text or listen as it is read aloud, marking places where they have questions.

Student Learning Objective: To clarify understanding of a text by making notes and asking questions about parts of a text that prompt confusion or curiosity

We recommend reading the selection aloud, if possible. Reading aloud:

- Allows students to enjoy the selection
- Helps students take in unfamiliar vocabulary
- Gives students the model of a fluent reader using appropriate pace and expression
- Ensures that all students begin their interpretive work on an equal footing
- Leads naturally to students sharing questions about the selection

Sharing Questions 15–20 minutes

Activity Summary: Students share questions about the text.

Student Learning Objectives: To identify questions arising from a text and to begin to identify interpretive questions

After the first reading, encourage students to ask any questions they have about the selection. Try writing students' questions on the board or chart paper. Factual or vocabulary questions can be cleared up at this point, while questions reflecting students' curiosity about the meaning of the selection should be noted and saved for Shared Inquiry discussion.

Sharing questions after the first reading:

- Teaches students that their curiosity is a starting point for interpretive thinking
- Develops the habit of reflecting and questioning after reading
- Clears up initial misreadings and comprehension difficulties
- Generates questions worth exploring in discussion
- Fosters a cooperative learning atmosphere
- Helps you gauge students' understanding of the text and identify interpretive issues of interest

Second Reading *(time depends on selection length)*

Activity Summary: Students reread the selection and mark passages using a specific note prompt. Then students briefly compare and discuss their notes.

Student Learning Objectives: To reread and mark passages for deeper understanding of a text and to explore different responses to a text by explaining and comparing notes

The activities in this guide include a note prompt that highlights a key interpretive issue in the text. In reviewing students' notes with them, look for opportunities to help students become aware of and compare different reactions to the same passage.

Rereading and taking notes:

- Gives students guided practice in choosing passages for close examination
- Develops students' ability to recall and use supporting evidence for their opinions
- Enables students to draw connections as they read and recognize interpretive issues
- Helps students see that a passage can have different interpretations
- Encourages students to use notes as a way of reacting to and thinking about literature

Tips for Sharing Notes

To help your students get the most out of making and sharing notes:

- Allow time for students to discuss some of their notes, so that they see different interpretive possibilities. With a longer text, ask students to share their notes from two or three pages.
- Ask students to share not only what they marked but also why they marked it, or have them discuss their notes in pairs while you circulate, asking follow-up questions as needed.
- Ask follow-up questions such as *Why did you mark the passage that way? Did anyone else mark it that way? Did anyone mark it differently, and if so, why?* to help students understand both their thinking and that of others.

Here are examples of how two students marked a page in the Declaration of Independence when asked to mark with an **R** assertions that seem **radical** and mark with an **SE** assertions that seem **self-evident**.

Student A

        We hold these truths to be self-evident, that <u>all men are created equal</u>, that they are endowed by their Creator with <u>certain unalienable rights, that among these are life, liberty and the pursuit of happiness</u>. That to secure these rights, governments are **R** instituted among men, <u>deriving their just powers from the consent of the governed</u>, That whenever any form of government **R** becomes destructive of these ends, <u>it is the right of the people to alter or to abolish it</u>, and to institute new government, laying its foundation on such principles, and organizing its powers in such form, as to them shall seem most likely to effect their safety and happiness. Prudence, indeed, will dictate that governments long established should not be changed for light and transient causes; and accordingly all experience hath shown that mankind are more disposed to suffer, while evils are sufferable, than to right themselves by abolishing the forms to which they are accustomed. But when a long train of abuses and usurpations, pursuing invariably the same object evinces a design to reduce them under absolute despotism, it is their right, <u>it is their duty, to throw off such government</u>, and to provide new guards for

SE Inherent rights
SE These are basic—it's assumed

Student B

        We hold these truths to be self-evident, that <u>all men are created equal</u>, that they are endowed by their Creator with certain **R** unalienable rights, that among <u>these are life, liberty and the pursuit of happiness</u>. That to secure these rights, governments are instituted among men, deriving their just powers from the consent of the governed, That whenever any form of government **R** becomes destructive of these ends, <u>it is the right of the people to alter or to abolish it</u>, and to institute new government, laying its foundation on such principles, and organizing its powers in such form, as to them shall seem most likely to effect their safety and happiness. Prudence, indeed, will dictate that governments long established should not be changed for light and transient causes; and accordingly all experience hath shown that mankind are more disposed to suffer, while evils are sufferable, than to right themselves by abolishing the forms to which they are accustomed. But when a long train of abuses and usurpations, pursuing invariably the same object evinces a design to reduce them under absolute despotism, it is their right, it is their duty, to throw off such government, and to provide new guards for

R
New idea!

Shared Inquiry Discussion 30–45 minutes

Activity Summary: Students explore the text's meaning by discussing an interpretive question.

Student Learning Objectives: To generate ideas in response to an interpretive question about a text; to support ideas and arguments with relevant evidence from the text; and to respond to the ideas, questions, and arguments of other students

In this cornerstone activity of all Great Books programs, students work together to interpret the text. Each Shared Inquiry discussion begins with independent thought: students write their own answers to an interpretive question that you pose as the focus of discussion. Then, guided by your follow-up questions, students discuss and develop their ideas, supporting their ideas with evidence from the selection.

The activities in this guide include questions for discussion. Focus questions—interpretive questions about key issues of meaning—appear in boldface type. We encourage you to use these in combination with questions generated by you or your students. Each focus question is followed by a group of related questions that can be used as follow-up questions to help students take a closer look at specific passages.

The following pages explain how to introduce students to and conduct Shared Inquiry discussion. Two handouts—Shared Inquiry Discussion Guidelines and Building Your Answer in Shared Inquiry Discussion—can be found at the back of this guide on pages 36–37 and 38–39, in reproducible format for your convenience.

Introducing Students to Shared Inquiry Discussion

To establish an atmosphere that promotes the lively exchange of ideas, arrange the room in a circle or square so that everyone can see and hear one another. If this isn't possible, encourage students to turn to look at the person talking, acknowledging one another and not just the teacher. Students should have a convenient surface for reading and writing.

To prepare students for Shared Inquiry discussion:

- Emphasize that in discussion you are not looking for a "right" answer, but are interested in exploring a question that has more than one reasonable answer based on the text. Because there is more than one reasonable answer, the objective is not to reach consensus but to help students develop their own ideas.
- Let students know that you will be asking them to explain their ideas, give evidence to support them, and respond to other students' comments.
- Encourage students to raise questions of their own and to talk to one another rather than always to you.
- Explain the discussion guidelines (pages 36–37) and the reasons for them. You may want to copy these pages for students or display the guidelines in the classroom.
- Distribute the Building Your Answer form (pages 38–39). Let students know that using the form will help them trace the progress of their ideas about a text while facilitating any writing you may assign after the discussion.

Leading Shared Inquiry Discussion

The following suggestions will help you lead the most productive Shared Inquiry discussions for your students.

Begin the discussion with a focus question and ask students to write down an answer. Review your students' questions, your notes, and the suggested questions in this guide to help you choose a focus question that has more than one reasonable answer and reflects your and your students' interests.

Giving students time before the discussion to reflect individually on the focus question lets them gather their thoughts and find evidence for their ideas. Having students write an answer on their Building Your Answer form gives them an excellent starting point for participating in the discussion and enables you to call on less vocal students knowing they have something to contribute. Students can also reflect on their answer after the discussion, considering how they have added to or changed their ideas in response to others.

Share your curiosity and enthusiasm by listening carefully and asking follow-up questions often. Your attentive listening and follow-up questioning drive and sustain effective discussion. Use follow-up questions to help students:

- **Clarify comments.** *What do you mean by that? Can you say more about that?*
- **Support ideas with evidence.** *What in the text gave you that idea? What did the author do or say that made you think so?*
- **Test and develop ideas.** *If you think that's what the author means, then why does he or she say this in the text? How does this passage in the text fit in with your idea?*
- **Respond to others.** *What do you think about what she just said? Do you agree with that idea? Does anyone have an idea we haven't heard yet?*

Return frequently to the text and the focus question. Keep the discussion grounded in the text by asking students to support their answers with evidence. Help students think about ideas in depth by asking them to explain how their comments relate to the focus question.

Encourage students to think for themselves and to speak directly to one another instead of just to you. This makes students responsible for discussion and fosters an environment of open inquiry and respect. Try to remain in the role of a neutral leader by only asking questions, and avoid answering questions or endorsing ideas with comments such as "Good idea" or "I like that."

Keep a record of the discussion. Using a seating chart to track students' participation will help you identify patterns of participation and assess students' contributions. You might make check marks next to students' names when they offer an answer and mark "NA" when a student has no answer when asked to speak.

End the discussion when your group has explored the focus question in depth. You can usually tell when your group has considered a number of answers to the focus question and most students could, if asked, provide their own "best answer" to it. You may wish to check by asking, *Are there any different ideas we haven't heard yet? Is there any other part of the text we should look at before wrapping up?* Remind students that they do not need to reach a consensus, because the text supports multiple interpretations.

Writing After Discussion

Activity Summary: Students write in response to a question or prompt about the text.

Student Learning Objectives: To develop a thesis in response to a text and support that thesis with appropriate evidence from the text and other sources; to extend students' thinking about the ideas raised in the selection

The activities in this guide include prompts for writing and reflection after discussion. After participating in Shared Inquiry discussion, students are well prepared to consolidate or extend their responses to a text in writing. In addition to writing on one of the topics in this guide, students can consult their completed Building Your Answer form and use their answer to the focus question as the thesis of an essay.

Writing after discussion:

- Gives students practice in systematically articulating, supporting, and developing their ideas
- Stimulates original thought and encourages students to connect what they read to their own experiences and opinions
- Helps students build a commitment to reading and critical thinking by continuing their thoughtful engagement with a selection's ideas

Assessment and Reflection

Assessment

If you assign a participation grade, keeping a seating chart will help you record students' oral work for later marking. Comparing your notes from week to week will help you give students feedback on their progress, individually or as a group.

The writing prompts lend themselves to extended written responses, which can be graded like other essays. You can also evaluate the written work students do in preparation for discussion, including their questions and notes, and their Building Your Answer in Shared Inquiry Discussion forms. You may wish to ask students to submit a portfolio of their written work on a selection of their choice or from selections covered over the course of the semester.

The Great Books Critical Thinking Rubric on pages 40–41 is a detailed outline of the critical thinking skills developed in Great Books programs. Applying the rubric to students' responses in discussion as well as to their written work will give you more complete and dependable information. To use the rubric to assess critical thinking, follow these steps:

- Prior to Shared Inquiry discussion, choose one to three students to assess. As your comfort level in leading discussions grows, you may wish to increase the number of students you assess.
- After the discussion, record notes about the thinking skills of those students you are assessing. Use the notes on your seating chart to recall discussion responses. (You may also wish to record the discussions for assessment purposes.)

- Flesh out your notes about each student by reviewing their written work, including the Building Your Answer form.
- Assign separate grades for idea, evidence, and response, or grade for just one objective. Due to the collaborative nature of Shared Inquiry, a student's contributions may pertain to only one area.
- Give students feedback by sharing the rubric with them and offering suggestions for improvement.

Reflection

To help students reflect on their own learning, after every two or three discussions ask them to share their thoughts on how the discussions are going and how they might be improved. Help the class set specific goals for improvement in areas such as supporting their opinions with evidence from the text, staying focused on the meaning of the text under discussion, and speaking directly to other students rather than just to the teacher.

Online Resources
- www.greatbooks.org/assessmenttools/ for grade-specific assessment tools
- www.greatbooks.org/links-for-teachers/ for teacher resources
- www.greatbooks.org/commoncore/ for more on how Great Books programs and the Shared Inquiry method meet Common Core State Standards
- www.greatbooks.org for additional assessment and reflection resources

Reagan's Farewell Address
Ronald Reagan

Prereading

Look at the picture of a city on a hill on page 47 of your book. What words or phrases come to mind when you view this picture?

Second Reading

Mark with an **A** places where you **agree** with what Reagan says about America; mark with an **D** places where you **disagree** with him.

Interpretive Questions for Discussion

Why does Reagan think of America as a "shining city upon a hill"?

1. Why does Reagan say that "America is freedom"? Why is freedom "fragile"?
2. Why does Reagan say that we have to remember what we did in order to know who we are as Americans?
3. How can "an eradication of the American memory" result in "an erosion of the American spirit"?
4. Why does Reagan say that the city on a hill that he pictures as America is "wind-swept"?
5. Why does Reagan describe people who are seeking freedom as "hurtling through the darkness" toward America?

Writing After Discussion

Have students write an essay, using evidence from the text, to support their answer to the focus question in discussion, or use one of the following:

1. How does Reagan's description of a city on a hill support his statement that America is freedom?
2. Reagan often spoke of the city on a hill as a metaphor for America. What is another metaphor that you think defines America and what America stands for?
3. Create and explain a metaphor that captures the true meaning of your school or home.
4. Read "Life in a City on a Hill" by Sarah Vowell. What would Vowell think of Reagan's characterization of John Winthrop as "an early freedom man"?
5. Would Reagan agree with Winthrop's idea of America as expressed by Vowell—a country "fervently devoted to the quaint goals of working together and getting along"?

Religious Tolerance in America
Richard Rodriguez

Prereading

Recall a time when you participated in or witnessed a religious ceremony outside your own religion. Did you feel welcome, or out of place? What were your reactions to the similarities or differences you noticed?

Second Reading

Mark with a **P** places where Rodriguez indicates that religious beliefs have a **positive** impact on society; mark with an **N** places where he indicates that religious beliefs have a **negative** impact on society.

Interpretive Questions for Discussion

According to Rodriguez, is the highest form of religious tolerance in America religious syncretism, or is it Americans of different religions living and working together harmoniously?

1. Why does Rodriguez describe the civilization that Americans may be forming as "daring and splendid"?
2. If it is true that "secular America has largely survived religious sectarianism," why is it that "some Americans may feel the need to assert this is what I believe, not that"?
3. Are we meant to view widespread "spiritual miscegenation" as desirable?
4. What does Rodriguez mean when he says that "the last concoction from the American melting pot" is religious?

5. Why does Rodriguez say that "the great wisdom of Catholicism in the Americas" was "its willingness to absorb indigenous spirituality even while it converted the Indian"?
6. Does Rodriguez think that religious syncretism is necessary for religious tolerance?

Writing After Discussion

Have students write an essay, using evidence from the text, to support their answer to the focus question in discussion, or use one of the following:

1. Is maintaining one's religious identity in America more important, less important, or just as important as maintaining one's ethnic, racial, or social identity?
2. Examine the pie charts on page 54. If Rodriguez is correct in his essay, explain how the pie chart for the United States would change in the next ten or twenty years.
3. Does your family celebrate a religious holiday in a way that incorporates practices from more than one religion? What are the different practices, and why has your family adopted them?
4. How has the First Amendment helped produce the "spiritual miscegenation" Rodriguez describes?

Give Me Liberty or Give Me Death!

Patrick Henry

Prereading

Would you be willing to sacrifice your life to fight for your rights?

Second Reading

Circle the words *hope* and *truth* wherever they appear in the speech. Then state Patrick Henry's argument in a sentence or two, using the words *hope* and *truth*.

Interpretive Questions for Discussion

What is the main reason Patrick Henry insists "we must fight"?

1. Why does Henry emphasize that he is speaking "freely and without reserve," and not holding back "through fear of giving offense"?
2. What does Henry mean when he says, "This is no time for ceremony"?
3. Why does Henry frame the problem he is addressing as "a question of freedom or slavery"?
4. Why does Henry think it necessary to say twice, "Let us not deceive ourselves"?
5. Why does Henry think the colonists are "invincible"? Why does he maintain that "a just God" will help the colonists find friends to win in battle?
6. Why would Henry choose death over the loss of liberty?

Writing After Discussion

Have students write an essay, using evidence from the text, to support their answer to the focus question in discussion, or use one of the following:

1. Why do people risk their lives in order to be free to make their own decisions?
2. Imagine you are speaking after Patrick Henry and do not share his views. Write a speech presenting arguments against Henry's insistence that the colonists have no choice but to go to war.
3. Write an essay evaluating the effectiveness of Patrick Henry's speech.

Declaration of Independence

Thomas Jefferson

Prereading

How would it change your life to live independently as an adult does? What does it mean to you to be independent?

Second Reading

Mark with an **R** assertions in the Declaration that you think are **radical**; mark with an **SE** those that you think are **self-evident**.

Interpretive Questions for Discussion

Are the signers of the Declaration motivated by a sense of moral outrage, or by individual self-interest?

1. Why do the signers of the Declaration say that "the laws of nature and of nature's God entitle them" to a separate and equal place among the world's nations? Why do they later claim the right to be free "by the authority of the good people of these colonies"?
2. Why do the signers want to proclaim to the world their reasons for declaring independence?
3. Why is "all men are created equal" the first truth that the colonists proclaim? Why do the colonists say that this equality is "self-evident"?
4. Why do the colonists maintain that their rights, "endowed by their Creator," are "unalienable"?

5. Why do the signers think it is their duty, as well as their right, to change their system of government?
6. Why do the signers appeal to the "native justice and magnanimity" of their "British brethren"?

Writing After Discussion

Have students write an essay, using evidence from the text, to support their answer to the focus question in discussion, or use one of the following:

1. Do any of the ideas in the Declaration still sound radical to you today? Why?
2. What idea or ideas in the Declaration strike you as especially American?
3. Is democracy stronger when Americans think of themselves as "one people" or as diverse peoples?
4. Read "What Makes a Government Legitimate?" by John Locke. How do Locke's ideas about freedom, equality, community, and the body politic appear in the Declaration?

THE FEDERALIST PAPERS
JAMES MADISON

Prereading

What does the term *checks and balances* mean to you, as applied to the United States government?

Second Reading

Mark with a **G** passages dealing with the need to balance the power of one part of the **government** against another; mark with an **I** passages dealing with the need to balance various **interests** within American society.

Interpretive Questions for Discussion

Why does Madison say that the "interior structure of the government" is the only way to maintain the necessary division of power among its departments?

1. What does Madison mean when he says, "The interest of the man must be connected with the constitutional rights of the place"?
2. Why does Madison state that "ambition must be made to counteract ambition"?
3. Why does Madison believe that "in republican government, the legislative authority necessarily predominates"?
4. Why is Madison certain that the larger the society, the more "duly capable" it will be of self-government? Why does he qualify this statement by saying, "provided it lie within a practical sphere"?

5. What does it mean to say that "justice is the end of government"?

Writing After Discussion

Have students write an essay, using evidence from the text, to support their answer to the focus question in discussion, or use one of the following:

1. Do you agree with Madison that government is "the greatest of all reflections on human nature"?
2. How can liberty be lost in the pursuit of justice?
3. Is a system of checks and balances preferable to majority rule?
4. Read "Objections to the Constitution" by George Mason. Do Mason's assertions about the different powers of the branches of government reveal fatal flaws in Madison's view that the proposed Constitution establishes appropriate checks and balances?
5. Compare Madison's assertion that the rights of the minority "will be in little danger from interested combinations of the majority" with Mason's view that a simple majority vote on issues of interstate commerce could ruin the economy of the five Southern States.

What Would the Founders Do?

Richard Brookhiser

Prereading

Is it more admirable for elected leaders in Congress and the executive branch to stick to their principles and positions, or to compromise?

Second Reading

Mark with an **SU** places where Brookhiser points out something of **substance** in the Founders' work; mark with an **ST** places where he notes something about their **style**.

Interpretive Questions for Discussion

According to Brookhiser, what is the "style of thought," the "way of working," the "stance" that we can always take from the Founders?

1. Why does Brookhiser say that perhaps we should question the founders less?
2. According to Brookhiser, how was politics the means by which the Founders "secured liberty . . . and every other public good"?
3. Does Brookhiser think that politics is a matter of substance, or of style?
4. What does Brookhiser mean by "promissory notes to principles"?
5. Why does Brookhiser emphasize that disagreement and contention were "as much a part of [the Founders'] legacy as their principles"? Why does he say that "mere ambition generates conflict"?

Writing After Discussion

Have students write an essay, using evidence from the text, to support their answer to the focus question in discussion, or use one of the following:

1. If "contention is as much a part of [the Founders'] legacy as their principles," what should be our attitude today toward presidential debates, negative political ads, one-issue candidates, or third- or fourth-party candidates?

2. Do you agree that politics is the only way to secure liberty and the public good?

3. What advice would you give to a friend who has to decide between sticking to his or her principles or compromising on an important issue? When, if ever, is it appropriate to compromise?

Why I Hate Politics. That Government Kind.

Marcy Massura

Prereading

Why do people become cynical about politics?

Second Reading

Mark with an **H** places where Massura is being **humorous**; mark with a **C** places where she is being **cynical**.

Interpretive Questions for Discussion

What does Massura mean when she says she is "too informed"?

1. Why does Massura differentiate governmental politics from other types of politics?
2. Why does Massura say that she should "do politics"? Why does she underline "I should" and put it in bold type?
3. Why does Massura say that she thinks more about what she would wear than what she would say if she were the president?
4. Why does Massura say that she is not "totally" foolish or ignorant? Why does she refer to herself as "jaded"?
5. Who does Massura blame more for the state of governmental politics: the political system or the politicians themselves?

Writing After Discussion

Have students write an essay, using evidence from the text, to support their answer to the focus question in discussion, or use one of the following:

1. Do Massura's cynicism and humor make you more, or less, inclined to believe her statements about politics and politicians?
2. Do you agree with Massura that only people who are starving for fame and attention seek public office?
3. What do you think motivates "the best and the brightest" people that Massura talks about? How would you change the political system to attract more of these people?

Why I'm Political

Margaret Cho

Prereading

What does it mean to "be political"? Do you think of yourself as political?

Second Reading

Mark with an **F** places where you think Cho is being **funny**; mark with an **S** places where she is **serious**.

Interpretive Questions for Discussion

Why does Cho say that being referred to as a "political comedian" feels "right" and "strong" to her?

1. According to Cho, how can society's insistence on the "invisibility" of minorities make her "hide from herself"?
2. Why does Cho believe that her fear of her Americanness being diminished because she is Korean is the result of society's "racist brainwashing"?
3. What does Cho mean when she says that going out of her way to prove she is an American doesn't support the idea of being an American?
4. Why does Cho call herself a racist? Does she take any responsibility for being a racist?
5. Why does Cho imply that being "apolitical" is not possible? Does she think it is not possible for her specifically, or for anyone?

6. Why does Cho think that her "very presence as an Asian American woman talking about race and sexuality" is a political statement?
7. What does Cho mean by "being political"? Why is being political an essential part of her life and, in the end, all she has?

Writing After Discussion

Have students write an essay, using evidence from the text, to support their answer to the focus question in discussion, or use one of the following:

1. Do you agree with Cho that society consistently and constantly disregards minorities?
2. Is Margaret Cho, as an American citizen, a typical example of "we the people," or is she atypical?
3. Why is it important, or unimportant, for you to "be political"?
4. How does prejudice and bigotry rot a person from within?

Shared Inquiry Discussion Guidelines

Come to the discussion with your book, a pen or pencil, a notebook, and an open mind. In Shared Inquiry discussion, everyone, including the leader, considers a question with more than one reasonable answer and weighs the evidence for different answers. The goal of the discussion is for each of you to develop an answer that satisfies you personally.

Following these guidelines will make for a better discussion:

★ **Read the text twice before participating in the discussion.** This ensures that everyone is prepared to talk about the ideas in the selection.

★ **Discuss only the text that everyone has read.** This keeps the discussion focused on understanding the selection.

★ **Support your ideas with evidence from the text.** This enables everyone to weigh textual support for different ideas and to choose intelligently among them.

★ **Listen to other participants, respond to them directly, and ask them questions.** Shared Inquiry is about the give-and-take of ideas, and speaking directly to other group members, not always to the leader, makes the discussion livelier and more authentic.

★ **Expect the leader to only ask questions, rather than offer opinions or answers.** The leader's role is to listen and ask questions in order to help participants develop their own ideas, with everyone, including the leader, gaining a new understanding in the process.

Copyright © 2012 by The Great Books Foundation

Building Your Answer
in Shared Inquiry Discussion

Name: _____

Selection: _____

Focus question: _____
_____
_____

Your answer before discussion (include something from the text that supports your answer): _____
_____
_____
_____
_____

How did the discussion affect your answer? Did it change your mind or provide additional support for your answer? Did it make you aware of other issues? _____

_____

_____

_____

Your answer after discussion: _____

_____

_____

What in the selection helped you decide on this answer? _____

_____

Great Books Critical Thinking Rubric

Performance Level		Idea: Generating an Interpretation
7	Extends Interpretation	Extends ideas to interpret text as a whole ♦ Identifies themes, author's perspective ♦ Goes beyond the question, widens the issues under discussion
6	Builds Interpretation	Elaborates on own idea ♦ Defines terms, explores implications ♦ Resolves inconsistencies
5	Explains Answer	Explains how an idea answers the question ♦ Relates actions, characters, statements to each other ♦ To clarify, spells out assumptions, relates them to the question
4	Understands Issues	Fully understands the interpretive issue ♦ Infers motives and causes, addresses the question directly ♦ To clarify, tells more about the answer
3	Recognizes Alternatives	Asserts a considered answer, aware of alternative ideas ♦ May hesitate between answers ♦ To clarify, paraphrases answer
2	Offers Simple, Quick Answers	Gives a quick, simple answer to the question ♦ All-or-nothing, snap judgment ♦ To clarify, repeats answer
1	Begins to Answer	Talks about the text without addressing the question

Copyright © 2012 by The Great Books Foundation

EVIDENCE: USING SUPPORT FROM THE TEXT	RESPONSE: LISTENING AND RESPONDING TO OTHERS
Brings together evidence from whole text • Uses both major incidents and subtle details • Compares and weighs evidence	Seeks out other students' ideas • Asks questions to clarify other students' ideas and suggests possibilities • Suggests support for others' ideas
Builds case from several different passages • Retraces process of thinking • Continues to add evidence during discussion	Incorporates other students' ideas and evidence • Agrees or disagrees with specific parts • Follows whole discussion
Explains how a passage supports an idea • Explores meanings, connotations for relevant words, phrases • Sees when evidence works against own idea	Explains and gives reasons for agreement and disagreement • Critiques or supports other students' ideas • Asks other students simple questions
Understands the need for evidence • Spontaneously looks back into the text • Focuses on relevant sentences	Understands and roughly summarizes other students' ideas • May be convinced by others • Follows other students' counterarguments
Supports an answer against an alternative answer • Locates relevant major passages • Reads or recounts whole passages	Recognizes alternative answers and agrees or disagrees simply
Tends not to volunteer support; offers support only when asked • Recalls major text facts • Considers answer self-evident	Reacts briefly or quickly to other students' answers without talking about them
May retell the story or give an opinion about something mentioned in the text	Allows others to speak without interrupting

Copyright © 2012 by The Great Books Foundation

Notes